HOW THEY MADE THINGS WORK!

THE GREEKS

Written by Richard Platt • Illustrated by David Lawrence

FRANKLIN WATTS
LONDON•SYDNEY

First published in 2009 by Franklin Watts

Franklin Watts
338 Euston Road
London NW1 3BH

Franklin Watts Australia
Level 17/207 Kent Street
Sydney NSW 2000

A CIP catalogue record is available from the British Library.

Dewey number: 609

ISBN 978 0 7496 7478 6

Printed in China

Franklin Watts is a division of Hachette Children's Books, an Hachette UK company.

www.hachette.co.uk

Editor in Chief John C. Miles
Art Director Jonathan Hair
Designer Matthew Lilly
Editor Sarah Ridley
Picture researcher Sarah Smithies
Additional artworks by John Alston

Picture credits:
AAA Collection: 16t, 19t, 27; Corbis: 16br; Jens Stolt / Shutterstock: 7tr; Kennan Ward / Corbis: 18; Kenneth V. Pilon / Shutterstock: 7bl, 7br; LM Otero / AP Photo: 14b; Losmi Chobi / AP Photo: 19c; Mary Evans Picture Library: 14t, 15; Matt Houser / Shutterstock: back cover, 22; Pascal Baril / Kipa / Corbis: 13; Paul Picone / Shutterstock: 7tl, 7bc, 7cr; Peter Connolly / akg-images: 16bl; Rob Sylvan / iStockphoto: 28; Science Museum / Science & Society Picture Library: 17t; Science Photo Library: 17b; Timewatch Images / Alamy: 19b; Werner Forman Archive: 7cr.

Contents

HOW THE GREEKS MADE THINGS WORK

Before there was a nation called Greece, the people of the islands and coasts of the blue Aegean fought for land and power. Living in tiny city-states, they shared little more than a language 3,000 years ago. Yet over the next 11 centuries, the Greeks built a mighty empire that reached east to Pakistan and south as far as Egypt. Technology helped them do this. Inventions such as the crossbow made Greek soldiers dangerous foes, and pulleys made their ships go farther and faster.

Shipping and travel

In fact, it was shipping – and travel – that inspired the most ingenious Greek ideas. Pulleys (left) multiplied mariners' strength, so they could haul bigger sails. Lighthouses kept Greek ships off the rocks. Greeks voyaging far from home gathered knowledge of distant lands, making possible the first "world" maps. When storms wrecked ships, divers salvaged their cargoes with the aid of another clever Greek invention: the diving bell. And the most complex machine of the ancient world – a kind of clockwork computer – grew from the observations of Greeks abroad. It predicted the movements of the stars and sun that guided sailors to distant ports.

Aquatic necessity

Ocean travel was a practical skill that Greeks had to do well, for wide seas separated their scattered cities. But on the whole, the ancient Greeks were not a very practical lot. They were much better at thinking up brilliant ideas than at getting them to work. For example, one Greek inventor, Hero, dreamed up steam power – but then used it to drive a toy.

Archimedean antics

Hero was one of the few Greek inventors whose name we remember. Another, Archimedes, is more famous still. Though he was a brilliant scientist and mathematician, Archimedes might have smiled at the cause of his fame. For he probably did not invent the spiralling water-lifting machine (above) named after him: he was simply the first to describe it!

MONEY

The Greeks did not invent money: their neighbours, the Lydians, deserve the credit for this. However, the Greeks were quicker to realise just how useful little round discs of precious metal could be. Their homeland was spread out across the coast and islands of the Aegean Sea. Coins gave them a quick and easy way to trade, to measure wealth and to move it round easily.

Market madness

Before they had money, Greeks bartered (swapped) goods. It wasn't convenient: someone with many slaves and not enough cattle had to find a cattle farmer needing slaves. Gradually, they began using pieces of metal that stood for things they exchanged often. A cow-shaped lump of copper, for instance, was worth a cow. People used lumps of gold and silver, too, but these needed weighing for each bargain.

Greeks bartered and traded in the agora (the market or meeting place).

A fistful of drachmas

Coins made everything easier. A government stamp on each one guaranteed that it contained a standard amount of silver. This meant that everyone knew how many coins it took to buy a cow – or a cauldron, or a slave. Greeks first made coins around 600 BCE. The main coin was the drachma, which meant "a handful". It was worth a handful of obols – six long sticks of copper used for money before coins. Greeks continued to use the drachma until 2002.

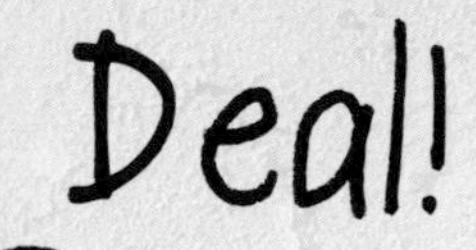

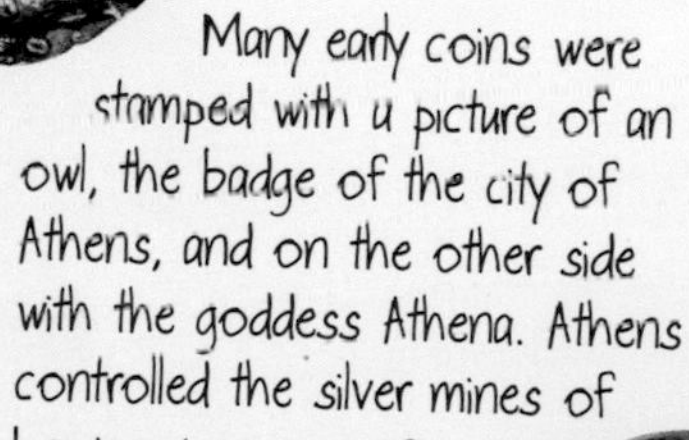

Many early coins were stamped with a picture of an owl, the badge of the city of Athens, and on the other side with the goddess Athena. Athens controlled the silver mines of Laurion (see page 10).

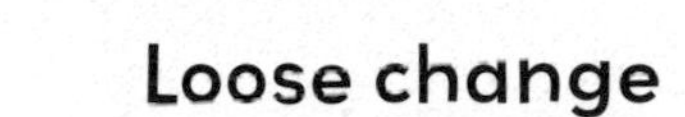

Loose change

One drachma was three day's pay for a labourer, so there were smaller coins for shopping and wages. Some were as small as fish scales and pin heads. Bigger coins, made of gold and worth up to 25 drachmas, were made for trading and banking. Their use helped to spread Greek money, power and influence along the whole Mediterranean coast.

What a talent

Before coins, Greeks exchanged heavy sheets of copper called talents. Most men could carry only one. Men who could lift more had "talent" – a word we still use to mean ability.

CITY PLANNING

Visit the remains of historic Greek cities today, and you might believe that their citizens lived in grand marble homes served by wide, clean roads. In fact, ancient Greek cities were foul, crowded, noisy places. Factories fought with homes for space and air. The streets stank of sewage, and dung heaps grew against house walls. Something had to be done.

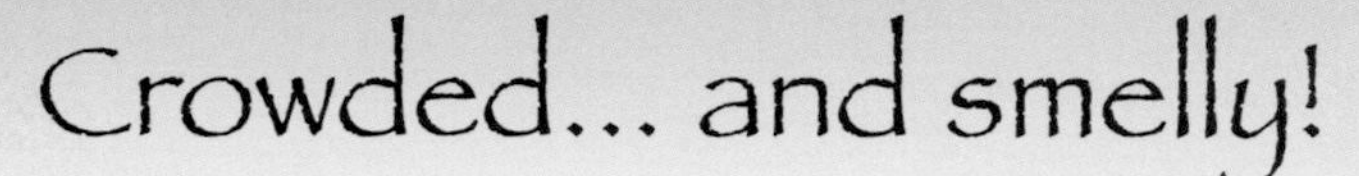

Crowded... and smelly!

Nobody planned old Greek cities. They just got bigger as more people moved in and built houses. There were no separate areas for business, worship, living and making things. Roads were often hardly wide enough for two people to pass. There were no sewers, and citizens openly used the streets as lavatories.

Planning more pleasant

It was impossible to change cities that already existed, but Greek architect Hippodamus realised that new cities could be much more pleasant places. In the 5th century BCE he became the world's first town-planner. He saw clearly that factories, houses, temples and markets all deserved their own places in different parts of the city. His ideas inspired today's zoning laws.

Babies and bathwater

The people of Athens threw absolutely everything they didn't want on the city's rubbish dumps. Even unwanted babies were left there to die! In villages everyone put up with this situation as there was more space, but in crowded cities the practice spread disease.

The Acropolis (a hilltop fort and temple) at Athens was magnificent, but overcrowded housing surrounded it.

Chessboard cities

Hippodamus' most famous achievement was Miletus, on the west coast of what is now Turkey. He planned the city on a grid. The agora (market square) and temples were at the centre. Streets crossed at right angles, and every house had a door onto the street (a novelty at the time).

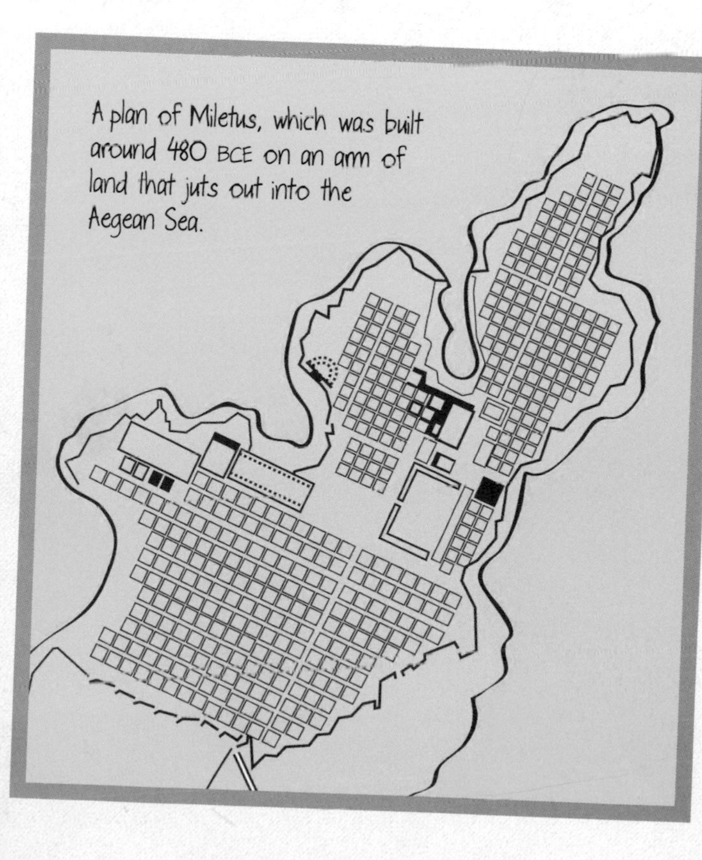

A plan of Miletus, which was built around 480 BCE on an arm of land that juts out into the Aegean Sea.

There's silver in them there hills!

MINING

Greeks needed metals. Tough and strong, metals like copper and iron were valuable materials for tools, weapons, armour and countless other uses. Above all other metals, though, the Greeks wanted silver to use in trade (see pages 6-7). They found it at Laurion, some 60 km (40 miles) southeast of Athens. There was plenty of silver there, but there was one problem: it was buried deep underground.

Digging into the hillside was easy, but the ore that miners extracted here did not contain very much silver.

Mine, all mine!

To get enough silver to make a modern pound coin, miners had to dig out 650 times as much ore (metal-rich rock). They began by cutting shallow caves in hillsides where red staining showed the rock was rich in metal. However, the richest ore lay much deeper. When miners sunk shafts to reach them, their tunnels collapsed, and the air soon became too stale to breathe.

Can you dig it?

The clever miners used several smart tricks to dig deeper and deeper. To stop their tunnels from crumbling, they left pillars of rock that held up the roof. They cut sloping shafts, so that they could carry the ore to the surface as if up a staircase. To make the suffocating atmosphere fresher, they lit fires at the bottom of shafts. The rising smoke drew in fresh air.

Deep diggers

The deepest mine shafts went down 117 metres (383 feet) – any lower and they filled with sea-water.

Working like a slave

Work in mines was dangerous and unpleasant. Some tunnels were just 0.6 m (2 ft) high. So the Greek's best idea of all was not to work in the mines themselves. Instead, they forced 20,000 slaves to dig out the silver at Laurion.

Tree tragedy

The silver was separated from the rock by smelting (heating to a high temperature). This used so much fuel that by the second century BCE the miners had cut down every tree in the region, and had to import charcoal by sea.

LIGHTHOUSE

Sailing a simple ship on the open sea has never been safe or easy. However, Greek ships heading for the harbour at Alexandria, Egypt, faced special dangers. Where the River Nile met the sea the coastline was flat. There were few easy-to-recognise landmarks, such as large buildings. Shipwrecks were common, and to stop them Egypt's governor in 3 BCE, Ptolemy, demanded action.

Zeus! Was that a rock?

When crossing the wide Mediterranean Sea, Greek mariners used stars to navigate (find their way). Even quite big mistakes didn't matter, because the water was deep. In shallow water closer to land, though, their navigation had to be more careful. They looked for familiar shapes on shore to guide them into harbour – but Alexandria lacked such landmarks.

Tall wonder

The Pharos became one of the Seven Wonders of the Ancient World. It stood for 1,700 years, until an earthquake toppled the tower in the 14th century.

Follow that beam!

Egypt's first Greek ruler, Ptolemy, asked Sostratus of Cnidus to find a way of guiding mariners into the port. The engineer and architect suggested building the world's first lighthouse. Called the Pharos, after the island on which it stood, the lighthouse was 28-storeys and 115 m (377 ft) high. Mariners could see its light when they were more than a day's sailing away.

According to legend, giant mirrors at the top of the Pharos reflected the light of a wood fire by night, and the sun by day.

Finding the Pharos

In 1994, 30 scuba divers led by marine archaeologist Jean-Yves Empereur (right) studied the sea-bed around Pharos Island in Alexandria harbour. They found hundreds of stone blocks. The later discovery of statues of Ptolemy and his wife suggests that the stones were the ruins of the famous lighthouse.

DIVING BELL

The Greeks have always been sailors. They had no choice: their nation includes some 2,000 islands. The Aegean and Mediterranean seas they sailed on are calm compared to the Atlantic Ocean, but shipwrecks were still a common and tragic occurrence. When valuable cargoes went to the bottom, they sent down divers to salvage them – bring them to the surface.

Diving bells were the only way to descend to wrecks until the 19th century.

Heavy breathing

Grasping stones to add weight, Greek divers swam down to shipwrecks, returning with whatever they could carry. Sailors on the ship above helped with heavy items by hauling the diver to the surface using a rope tied around his waist. However, without modern scuba apparatus, a diver could stay underwater only as long as he could hold his breath.

Modern breath-hold divers use fins to guide their descent. Ancient Greek divers instead used flat rocks. These dragged them quickly down, and turning them steered the diver like a ship's rudder.

Airheads

Some time before the 4th century BCE, Greek divers had figured out how to take a supply of air down with them to the sea-bed. They lowered huge metal pots, or bells, into the water, trapping air inside them. When divers could hold their breath no longer, they could swim into the bell and gulp in lungfuls of the trapped air. It was 2,000 years before anyone found a better way for divers to breathe underwater.

A metal bell of air, 1.5 m (5 ft) wide, could help keep two divers underwater for 20 minutes at a time.

Depth demons

Greek salvage divers were paid according to their breath-holding ability: the deeper they could dive, the more money they earned.

Alex in a fish bowl

Legends tell that Greek general, Alexander the Great, was lowered in a glass bell to watch divers at work in 322 BCE. The artist who painted this 16th-century picture of the event had a vivid imagination: making a glass vessel this big was impossible in Alexander's time!

It's a toy, Hero!

STEAM POWER

Lifting and shifting stuff was easy in ancient Greece, because there was plenty of power. It didn't come from electricity or motors, but from muscles and wind. On land the Greeks depended on the strength of slaves and animals; sail power helped at sea. So perhaps it's not surprising that when they invented steam power, they didn't really know how to make use of it!

Slave power

Slaves, the main power supply for Greece, made up about a third of the population. The property of free Greeks, slaves were foreign prisoners-of-war, or had lost their freedom because they owed money. Often whipped to work, they really did move mountains at the Laurion silver mines (see pages 10-11). Mules and oxen sometimes helped them; on ships the sails gave slaves some rest.

Greek sailors harnessed the wind to power ships – even galleys had sails.

Lines of slaves pulled on oars to power along huge Greek galleys.

On land, oxen pulled carts or ploughs. Some Greek farmers continued to use oxen until fairly recently.

Steam spinner

Steam power could have saved Greek slaves and beasts a lot of back-breaking work. It was the invention of engineer Hero (he didn't have another name) who lived in Alexandria, Egypt, in 1 CE. Hero boiled water in a tightly sealed cauldron. He fixed a couple of pipes on top, and between their bent ends he suspended a metal ball. Steam flowing up the pipes and into the ball flew out through angled jets, setting the ball spinning.

Hero's invention, the aeolipile, worked rather like a modern lawn sprinkler. This is a reconstruction.

Close, but no prize

Hero was clever, but he didn't spot the real value of his invention. He treated it as a toy. Really useful steam engines were not invented for another 1,600 years.

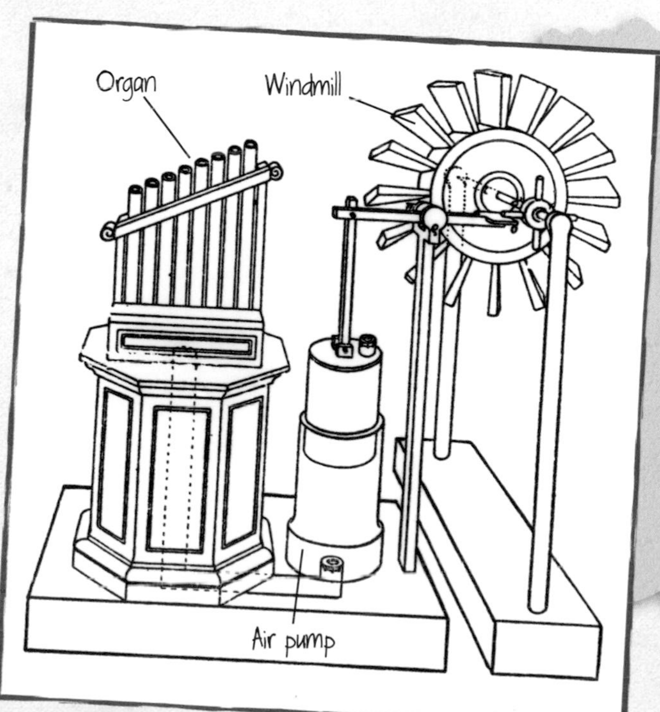

Hero's windmill looked like a child's windmill-on-a-stick.

Missed again...

Hero also found a new source of power for an old device – the pipe organ. Invented 300 years earlier by Greek engineer Ctesibius, it used water to pump air through long pipes to make musical notes, played from a keyboard. Hero pumped the organ from a windmill, but overlooked a much better use for its powerful sails: grinding corn.

COMPUTER

What could be more modern than a computer? Certainly, electronic computers with discs and chips belong to the 20th century, but the Greeks got there first. Their computers were made of sheets of bronze, carefully filed into intricate cogwheels. Wound up like clocks, they could predict the movements of the moon, stars and planets.

Heavens above!

The twinkling, starry night sky meant a lot to the Greeks. They used it to navigate, as a calendar, to set the dates of festivals, and even (superstitiously) to foretell the future. But the heavens, and especially the planets, moved in a baffling way.

"Can you see it?"

To make it easier to spot special stars, Greek astronomers imagined them in patterns, called constellations. They named each one after people or objects with similar shapes, such as Aquarius, the water-carrier, or Canis, the dog.

Mechanical marvel

About 2,100 years ago, brilliant Greek astronomers and mechanics built a cogwheel computer to work out how the heavens moved. Its 30-or-so gears could look ahead 54 years, predicting eclipses (sun, Earth and moon alignments) and the times when stars appeared. Lost in a shipwreck, the computer (right) was rediscovered in 1900, and named the Antikythera Mechanism after the island closest to the wreck site.

Researcher Bob Deroski made this working model of the mechanism for the Archaeological Museum in Athens.

Mistaken mechanism

Nothing as smart as the Antikythera Mechanism was made until the clocks of 14th-century Europe. Scientists who first studied it could not believe ancient Greeks made it. They thought it must have fallen overboard from a more modern ship.

Get in gear

The perfection of the Antikythera computer amazed scientists. Before its discovery, they had thought that the Greeks only knew how to use crude gears to move power around, or change its direction. For instance, in this picture, a bull pulls a wheel around. Gears carry the rotation to another shaft that drives a corn mill and a grindstone for sharpening knives.

PULLEYS

It's a ropey idea!

"One, two, three, HEAVE!" Without this command, no sailing ship would ever get to sea. When they heard it, Greek mariners strained every muscle to pull on the ropes that raised sails or anchors. It was enormously hard work – until a clever Greek found a way to halve or even quarter the effort required. The pulleys he devised found a use on land, too – making the gods fly!

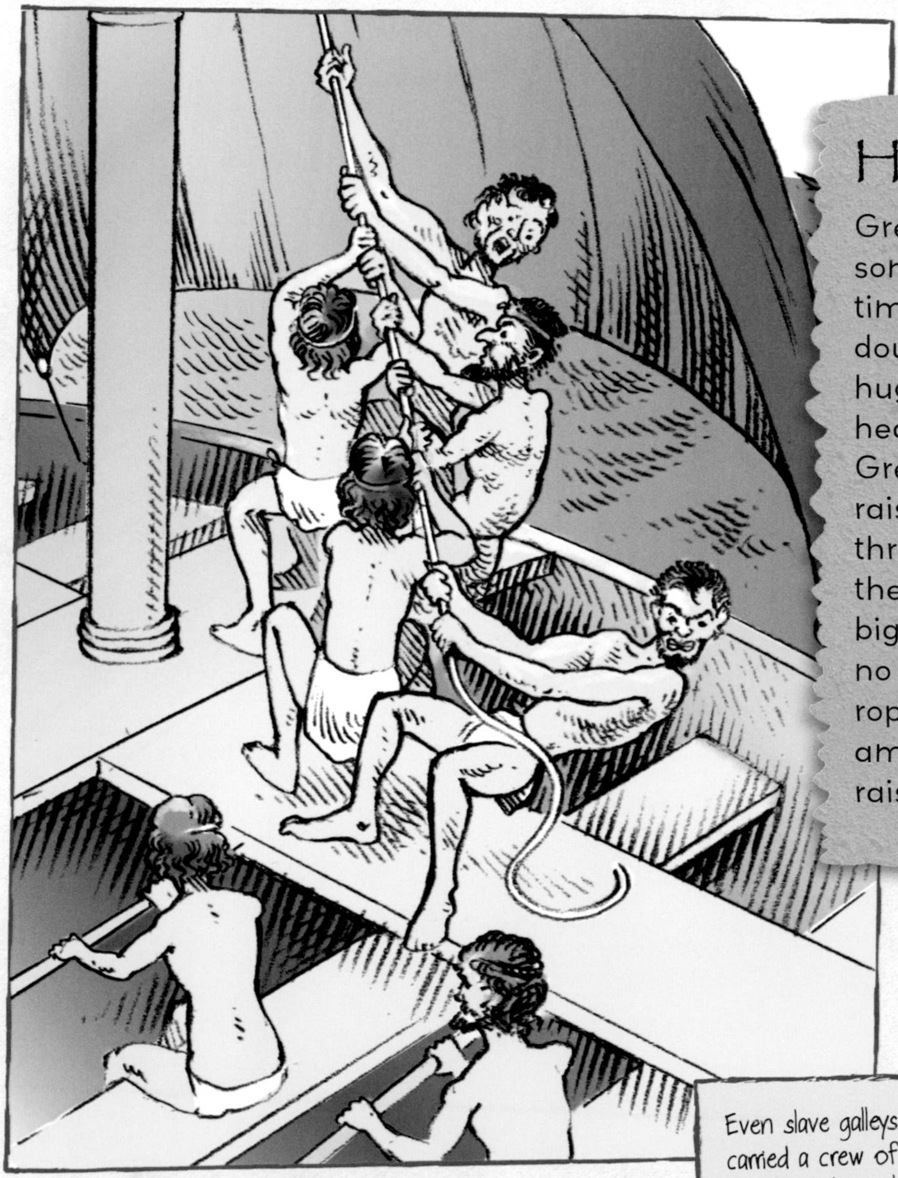

Haul away

Greek ships were big – some were more than four times the length of a double-decker bus. Their huge sails were immensely heavy. On small, early Greek ships, the ropes raising the sails just ran through a hole at the top of the mast. As ships got bigger, this simple system no longer worked. The ropes stuck fast. No amount of pulling could raise the heavy sail.

Even slave galleys rowed by oars carried a crew of ten mariners to adjust the sails.

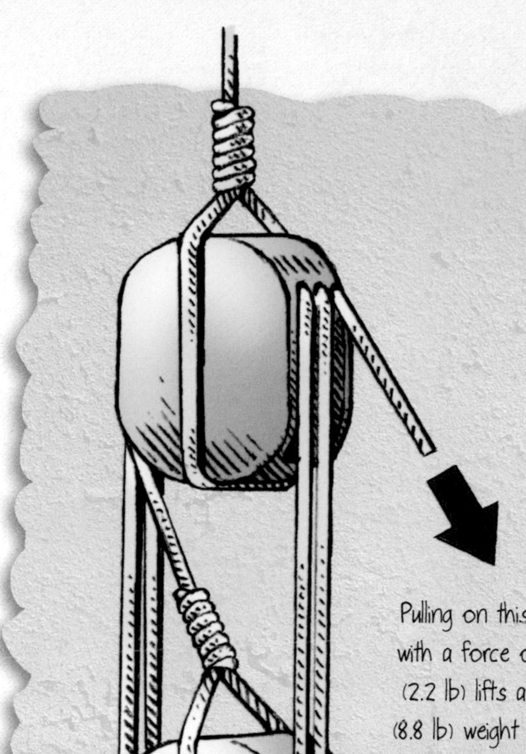

On the pull

Passing the rope over a wheel, called a pulley, cut down the friction (rubbing). Adding a second wheel created what we now call a block and tackle. This had the almost magical effect of reducing by half the pulling needed – a smaller force was exerted over a longer distance. Where before it took four sailors to raise a sail, now two could do it. Adding more pulleys made the job easier still.

Pulling on this rope with a force of 1 kg (2.2 lb) lifts a 4 kg (8.8 lb) weight below. However, sailors must also pull the rope four times as far.

The invention of the block and tackle allowed the Greeks to make far bigger ships with huge sails.

Look, no water!

Archimedes, in 3 BCE, bragged that with pulleys he could move any weight. He proved it by dragging along the ground a long ship, *Syracusia*, fully laden with freight and passengers.

Flying gods

Pulleys came in handy in Greek theatres, too. When a play called for a god to appear, stage hands lowered an actor "from the heavens". In fact, he was supported by ropes and pulleys and lowered from a crane (right).

Flying gods impressed Greek audiences, just as special effects stun us in the cinema today.

CRANE AND WINCH

The Parthenon is a temple dedicated to the Greek goddess Athena.

Towering high over the skyline of the Greek capital, Athens, the Parthenon is one of the greatest buildings of the ancient world. Constructing it in the 5th century BCE involved shifting huge stone blocks and lifting them more than 10 m (34 ft) above the ground. Cranes and winches enabled Greek masons to raise the stones and position them precisely.

Muscly masons

All stone is dense stuff, but the marble that Greek architects preferred is heavier than most. A 30 cm (1 ft) cube of it is about the most a man can lift without help. For small buildings, Greek masons could shift blocks by sliding them up ramps, or by placing rollers underneath them. Lifting them into place, though, demanded many masons with massive muscles.

Jumbo blocks

The heaviest blocks at the top of the Parthenon weighed nine tonnes – as much as an adult African elephant.

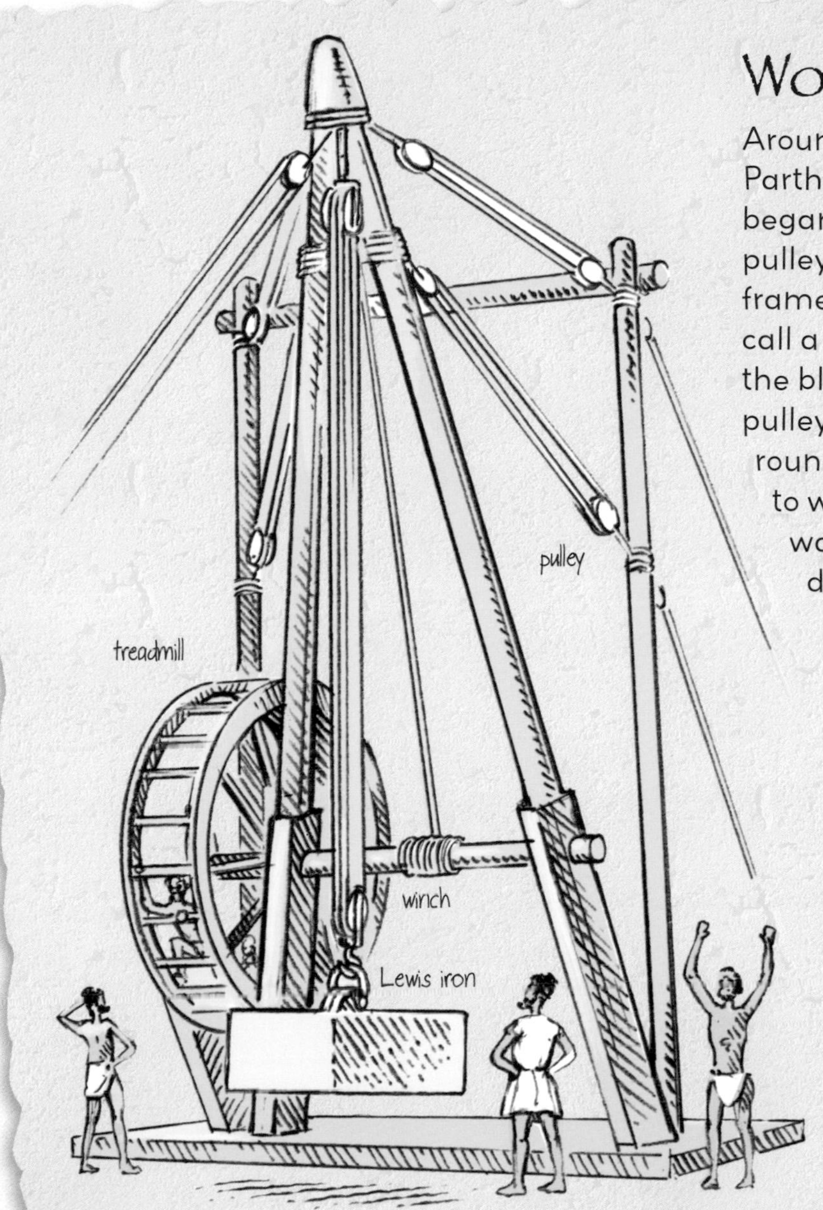

Wonderful winch

Around the time that the Parthenon was built, Greek masons began to lift stone blocks using pulleys (see previous page). A frame of heavy timbers that we'd call a crane held up the pulleys and the block they lifted. Rope from the pulleys ran to a winch. This was a round timber that masons turned to wind up the rope. Turning it was a lot easier than pulling directly on the rope. To grip and lift the blocks, masons cut specially-shaped holes in the stone and fitted in Lewis irons (see below).

Turning the winch by having a slave walk in a treadmill, one mason could easily lift a five-tonne block.

Lewis irons

Three carefully-shaped pieces of metal made a quick-release bracket for lifting stone.

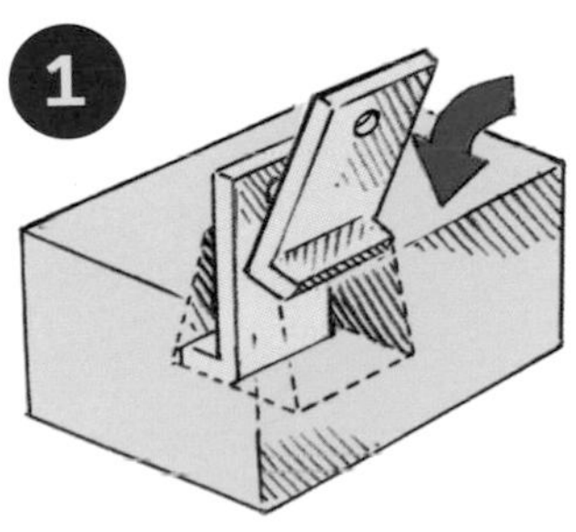

Pair of metal "L"s fit into wedge-shaped hole.

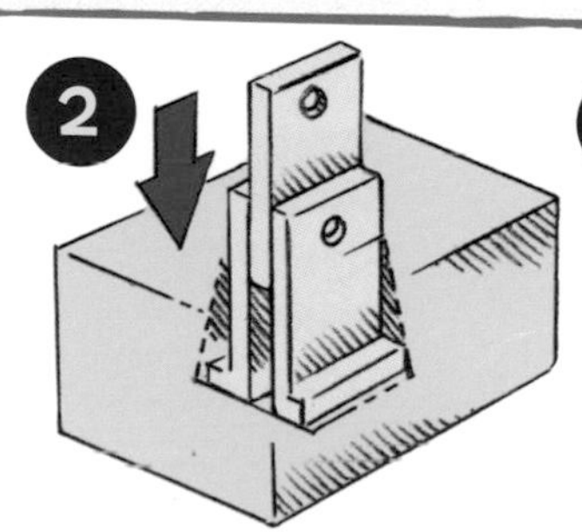

Sliding in a flat plate locks them in place.

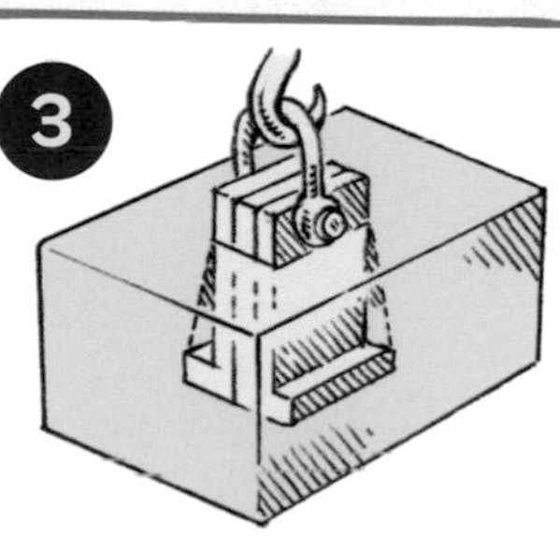

Bar through the holes makes lifting easy.

That's a magic spiral!

SCREW THREAD

Wound around a column, a rope or a ribbon traces a spiral pattern that is pretty, but hardly useful. However, cut a groove to follow the spiral and the column turns into an amazing machine. It becomes a screw: a simple device that presses powerfully forward when it's turned. Invented by engineer Archytas of Tarentum in the 4th century BCE, the screw allowed Greek farmers to squeeze more oil from olives, and juice from grapes.

Squashy problem

Extracting the highly-prized oil from a crop of olives wasn't easy. Greek farmers piled up baskets packed with the ripe berries, then squeezed them using a long lever slotted into a hole in the wall. Even with heavy weights – and the farmer – on the other end, it was impossible to squeeze out all the oil.

With a simple beam press four men could extract 275 kg (600 lb) of oil in a day.

Amazing olive

Olive oil gave Greeks a third of their energy. They also burned it in lamps and made it into perfume!

Turn of the screw

Nobody knows quite how Greek carpenters cut the first spiralling threads, but they had certainly managed this difficult task by the late 3rd century BCE. Fitting these giant wooden screws to olive presses allowed farmers to extract more oil, and do it with less effort. A single turn on the long levers crushed the olives with far more power than the heaviest weight.

The basic design of the screw press was the same for both olives and grapes.

Pumped up

The Greeks named quite a different kind of screw after inventor Archimedes of Syracuse, who lived in 3 BCE. His screw was a simple pump used to drain mines or water fields.

The lower end of the Archimedes' screw rested in a pool of water; the spiral screw inside lifted the water to the top end when workers turned the tube.

My bow's more powerful than YOUR bow!

CROSSBOW

Greek warriors faced a deadly and determined foe when they attacked Motya, Sicily, in 398 BCE. Their enemies were brave, well-organised fighters. Ordinary arrows glanced off their shields and helmets. However, the Greeks had a secret weapon: the "gastraphetes" or crossbow. With three times the power of an ordinary bow, it helped the Greek attackers to capture the city.

Bows for the boys

Greek archers pulled back the strings of ordinary wooden bows with just one hand. Even the strongest could not pull a string harder than about 27 kg (60 lb). This limited the power and range of their arrows as they could not pierce quite thin metal armour. So most Greek soldiers fought with spears, not bows.

Once an archer had pulled back the string on an ordinary bow, he had to quickly aim and fire it.

Top twangers

It's not clear who invented the crossbow – Greek historians credit Zopyros, Archimedes, Ctesibius and others. What is clear is how much more powerful it was than ordinary bows. To draw back the string, an archer rested one end on the ground. The other end pressed against his chest or belly, giving the weapon its name. He pulled back the string by pressing forward with all his strength. This meant that the arms of the bow could be made of springy horn instead of wood, giving the bow three times the power.

Wicked weapon

The secret of the gastraphetes was a sliding bar that pulled back the bow-string as the archer pushed on it. A ratchet (hooked bar) stopped the bar from springing forward. Once the string was tight enough, the archer loaded an arrow and took aim. Pulling the trigger released the string, firing the arrow.

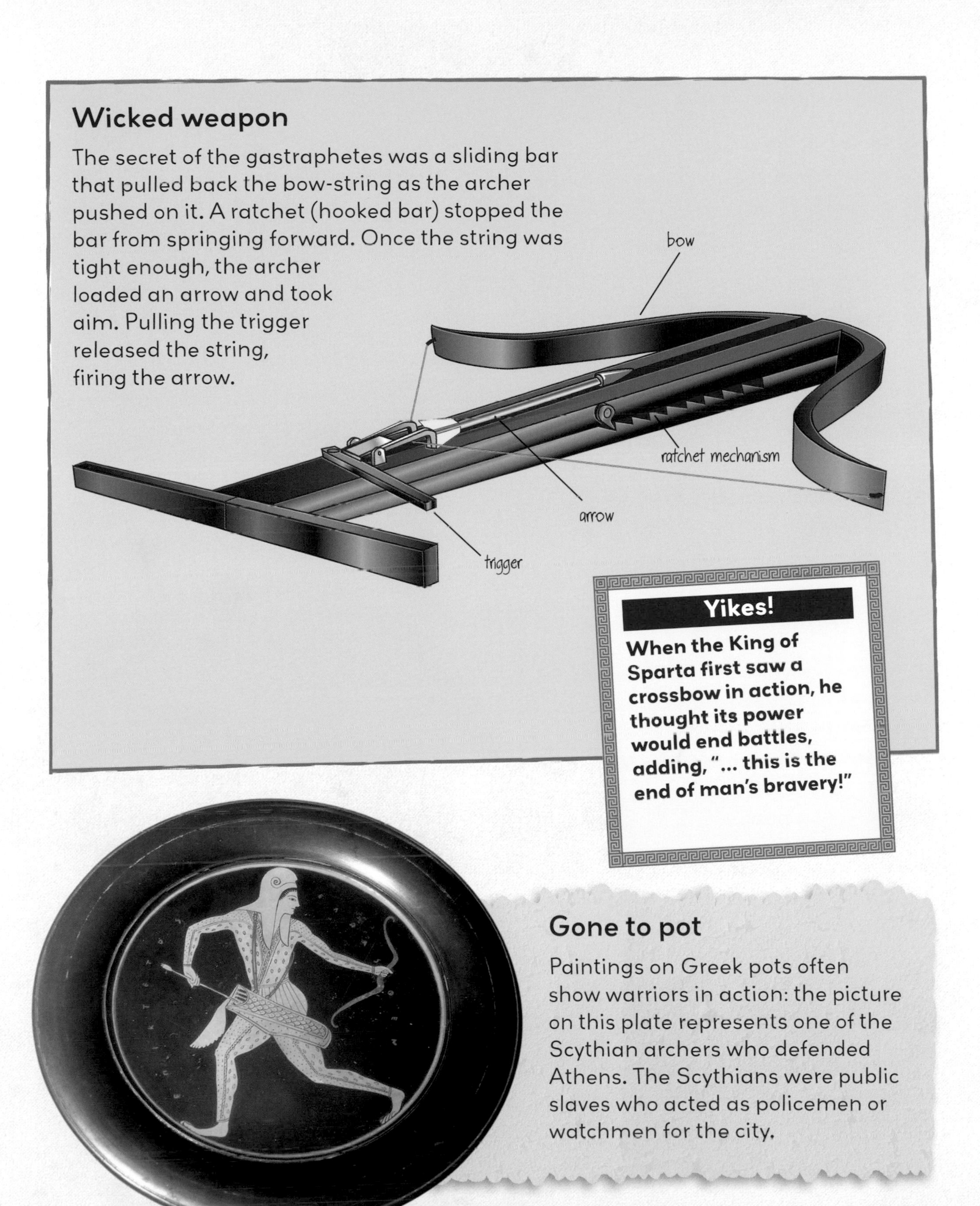

Yikes!

When the King of Sparta first saw a crossbow in action, he thought its power would end battles, adding, "... this is the end of man's bravery!"

Gone to pot

Paintings on Greek pots often show warriors in action: the picture on this plate represents one of the Scythian archers who defended Athens. The Scythians were public slaves who acted as policemen or watchmen for the city.

MAP

Fools!
Everyone knows
the world's flat!

Fly in a plane and you can understand a traveller's map immediately. Towns, roads, hills and lakes shrink and flatten until you feel you could fold up the land and put it in your pocket. However, the people of the ancient world had their feet firmly on the ground. To them, the idea of a map was not so obvious.

Thinking travellers

The Greeks were great travellers. Their voyages around the Mediterranean and Aegean seas made them think hard about their world, and its shape and size. They could not look down on the Earth's surface, as we can, so they had to be ingenious in their studies of geography.

Round Earth

Greek sailors knew the world was round. If it was flat, far-off things would just look smaller than those nearby. Instead, as they sailed the gently curving sea, distant things seemed to sink beneath the waves. The beach disappeared first, then tall things like trees. Mountains vanished last. Greek philosopher Aristotle in the 4th century BCE found proof of the Earth's round shape in an eclipse: the sun cast a rounded shadow of our planet on the moon's surface.

First world maps

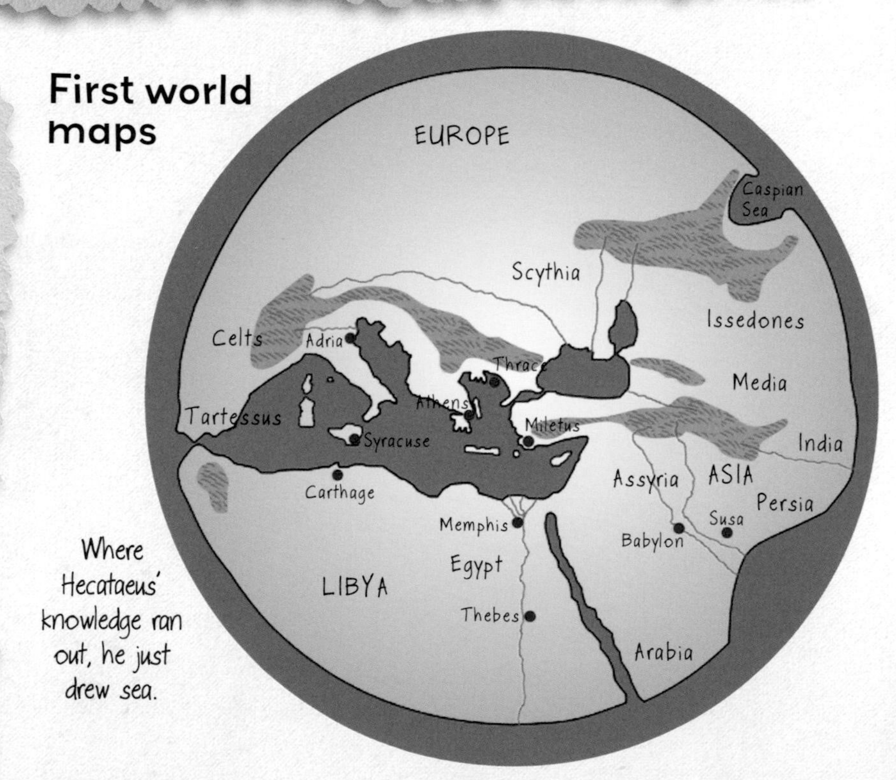

Two philosophers from the city of Miletus mapped the world first. Anaximander in the 6th century BCE and Hecataeus a century later both drew the world as a disc. They got the shape of the Mediterranean about right because they knew it well. The Black and Red seas were in the right place, too.

Mathematical measurer

Greek mathematician Eratosthenes worked out the circumference of the Earth in 3 BCE. He calculated 39,700 km (24,668 miles). We now know it's about 40,100 km (24,902 miles), so he wasn't far out!

How did he do it?

Eratosthenes knew that at midsummer in Syene, Egypt, the sun was directly overhead at noon, because it shone straight down a water well there.

On the same day he measured the sun's noon angle at Alexandria, about 787 km (490 miles) to the north. It was one fiftieth of a circle (about 7.2 degrees). Multiplying 787 by 50 (and adding a bit for luck) gave him his answer.

GLOSSARY

agora Open space in Greek cities where people met to debate or to hold markets.

archer Warrior armed with a bow and arrows.

architect Someone who designs buildings.

astronomer Scientist who studies the stars.

barter Exchanging goods for different products or materials, rather than for money.

BCE Before current era: equal to BC (before Christ) in the Christian calendar.

cargo Load carried by a vehicle, especially a ship.

cauldron Large pot, often used for cooking.

cogwheel Wheel edged with cogs (pegs or teeth) which allow it to turn another similar wheel.

constellation Group of stars in the sky, often named by ASTRONOMERS after objects their arrangement resembles.

copper Soft, orange-coloured metal that is easily shaped into tools or weapons.

dung Solid waste dropped from an animal's gut.

eclipse When the sun lines up with the moon and Earth (or another planet) so that one casts a shadow on another.

engineer Someone who uses their scientific knowledge to design or build useful things.

freight Transport of goods, especially by sea.

galley Large ship powered mainly by oars.

gear COGWHEEL, or a collection of linked cogwheels.

heavens The skies above us, and the sun, moon and stars we see in them.

landmark Object on the coast that can be seen easily from ships at sea, and used by sailors to judge their position.

lever Rotating arm or bar used to make lifting easier, or to turn a small movement into a large one.

Lydians People from the ancient region of Lydia, now southwest Turkey.

mariner Sailor.

mason Worker who cuts and lays the stones used in buildings.

nation Group of people living in the same region under a single ruler or government.

navigation Art and science of finding the way, especially at sea.

noon Time of day when the sun is at its highest and hottest.

ore Rock containing metal.

ox Cow or bull often used to pull a cart or plough.

press Machine used to squeeze fruit or seeds to extract their juice or oil.

salvage Recovering the sunken CARGO of a wrecked ship.

scuba Short for "self-contained breathing apparatus" – an air supply for swimming underwater.

Seven Wonders of the Ancient World List of amazing attractions around the Mediterranean Sea, used by ancient Greeks like a modern tourist guide. The list included the Great Pyramid and Pharos lighthouse in Egypt.

sewage Liquid and solid waste from the human gut and bladder.

sewer Trough or pipe to carry SEWAGE.

shaft Deep narrow hole in the ground, dug straight down.

slave Captive worker, kept as the property of a free person.